The poems in *Science Fiction Saint* explore themes of childhood, memory, family and sexuality in a language that succeeds in finding the space between a more traditional use of lyric line and the experimental use of form and language.

Science Fiction Saint

Nancy Jo Cullen

Leslie's mom,
you asked a poet and ended
up with a series.
Please enjoy
Nancy Jo Cullen
April 2002

FRONTENAC HOUSE
Calgary

Cover and Book Design by EPIX Design Inc.
Cover Illustration by Sam Weber.

Frontenac House acknowledges the support of Alberta Foundation for the Arts.

National Library of Canada Cataloguing in Publication Data

Cullen, Nancy Jo.
  Science fiction saint

(Quartet 2002)
Poems.
ISBN 0-9684903-7-9

I. Title. II. Series.
PS8555.U473S34 2002   C811'.54   C2002-910154-9
PR9199.3.C765S34 2002

Printed and bound in Canada

Published by Frontenac House Ltd.
1138 Frontenac Avenue S.W.
Calgary, AB   T2T 1B6   Canada
Tel: (403) 245-2491 Fax: (403) 245-2380
E-mail: editor@frontenachouse.com
Website: www.frontenachouse.com

1 2 3 4 5 6 7 8 9   06 05 04 03 02

To J

Acknowledgements

The League of Canadian Poets' Mentoring Programme in 1996/97 was key to the development of this book. Working with Erin Mouré (whose rigorous attention helped me to shape this book) was a tremendous learning experience. I am grateful to both the League and Erin for the opportunity. I would also like to thank Claire Harris and Fred Wah for great workshop experiences that contributed enormously to my development as a writer. I would like to thank The Canada Council for the Arts for their financial support during the writing of the manuscript. Finally, I would like to thank my partner Josette for her friendship and support through thick and thin and Mark for pitching in whenever asked.

Earlier versions of these poems have appeared in *Secrets From The Orange Couch*, *Blue Buffalo*, *CU2*, *Grain*, *Filling Station* and *New Quarterly*.

Contents

fortune smiles

fortune smiles

tonight in her pink satin sears dress in her pink satin mules
fortune is a photograph on her way to a party. look how she
hugs the arm of summer. how she shows off her legs. tonight
fortune will forget she has too many children. she will flash
her white toothed baby you better think twice before you
grab my ass smile. fortune laughs. she says luck you are a big
boy in a small town. she dances away from his careless feet.
serendipity gleams on her shoulders. it stinks of sweat and
too much coffee.

damage

I suppose it's true
we might be safer alone
I realize how little I know of tender after all it's a dog eat dog
world and I've been slashing from my little corner like once I
had this dream of anger escaping from my mouth   a
horror movie flying and slapping but isn't that how damage
goes
like the turn of a wind you couldn't predict
ripping you out so you are left
with the frame of a house no roof   I should say keep
your distance from my hurricane love because damage is the only
thing I've ever trusted could happen   I've made a poor refuge
of damage and damage won't hold you   I just think that
maybe together we can learn the possibilities of tender
we could fight back
not each other
but what took us here so quickly

indian paint brush

blood and grass nip at the ankles of children
in the woods all is love and war going on
fingers and secrets
dads are shining black oxfords because sunday's still a day off
  and there might be a barbecue
moms are always waiting

a girl is held down and humped by three boys
all their eyes have boners
rubbing between her breasts
during dishes before the graveyard shift when moms' and dads'
  eyes are on the mirror her skin becomes calyx
they don't see her there

on the back on an envelope pilfered from the trash
she draws the landscape with her blood
intangible trees
a picture of the day when she was a wicked girl and her mother's
  slap left a crimson bract on her cheek
she shouldn't be late

her father is flipping burgers for the kids
the girl sips her mother's gin and pink lemonade
homesick and mute
summer is peeling her shoulders and everyone is laughing
  because it's warm and they have potato chips
it's the time of their lives

girl dreams

boys dream of some greatness

they burp on command and drive their cars fast
when you put on your seat belt they say why
every night your mom sits in her chair waiting for you to
come home

girls dream of some boy

the reach of remembering over time
boys' torpid fingers insisting
you have been unaware girl when caution has been in order

girls dream of some boy
wake up with the dark ringing in their ears
sweat beading necklaces

you want to be a nurse or a saint   you want to be a teacher
you know by the time you are 25 you will have a   and a
you will be a   with hair that flips up at your shoulders just

do you know what getting nailed is?

you are always 9 always 16 always on the honour roll always fired
you are a science fiction saint
possibly because you were bottle fed rather than nursed from
the breast

boys dream of some greatness
what invokes such prodigious slumber
perhaps a company car

surprised by what you are reminded of in slender moments
time starved for attention
at work that afternoon you understand: everything ever
happens at once

they're watching through cracks in the fence
you still without breasts & too old to go topless
running through water

because last night you dreamt of some boy and
his name was dennis
it's likely he saw his father hit his mother
each night she is slapped again in that dream when dennis
whispers

do you know what getting nailed is?

alar

I want to be a bird
to know only   north in the summer south in the winter
like rich folks from kelowna with houses on the lake and a love
for jesus that's sex

uncomplicated urgencies:

> pee
> eat
> sleep
> perhaps fuck (if you're a bird)

otherwise
we meet because a knows b who left c who was a's best friend and
what's really interesting is
a and b's grandfathers were in grade 5 together and no one
knew that until b dated c
who was a's best friend only now nobody is speaking

> displaced
>   desire

> detour

flying over the tops of cars   over tangled pedestrians
perfect as the wind
bird swallows the sky
spits out heaven
names herself jesus

death & the maiden

(pocket full of icicles)

she never stands still enough
see
the maiden unfolding
first thighs and then
violins
shivering & summer
she bites the thought off
reaches into cool pockets
the maiden can't stay away
this feeling
pushing towards her mouth
is not what the maiden is told to

O
that death
that pretty little only object of her affection
makes a good opera   a great movie   a lovely piece of
should not be called upon this afternoon the maiden is
more than great art
her skin is whispers
sticks fingers in nobody's business
brava
brava
encore

being very happy

when i was 7 i had a dollar and i went to the Saan store and bought
a tank top for 49 cents and rubber thongs for 29 cents   i
spent 78 cents and still had change   i wore that top until i
couldn't   (you would say divide that up into 4 years that means
you spent 12 cents/year   you got a good deal)

when i was 7 i was a girl with a pixie cut who could be mistaken
for a boy   i had flawless skin and teeth that were bigger
than my mouth when i was 7 i felt   the kind of happiness
described in novels where you keep waiting for something
funny to happen but the author went somewhere else   i didn't
worry about wasting such an abstract thing as time   or how a
baby can suck love and hours out of your day   and it was like
that even before dennis the rapist and his friend whose name i
can't remember

i wonder if it nags at the back of their minds that afternoon they
were so terrible and 14 or if they routinely beat their wives and
children as a testament to their lives   and maybe they are
neither good nor bad   each day they drive their trucks to work
and home again   smoking and singing along to Hank Williams
Jr. or the Steve Miller Band   perhaps they have forgotten their
adolescent experiment with rape

i learned something about boys that afternoon but it wasn't the
worst thing my childhood taught me and don't ask me what the
worst was   i can't remember   when i was 7 i never made the
same mistake twice

when i was 7 the first thought that went through my head was
be a good girl now   but it didn't go through my head like that
it went like this:
do you want me to give you something to cry about

when i was 7 there was a scab on my elbow that lifted off in one
complete piece like the top of a cupcake   who would have
guessed it would bleed so much

l'air du temps

personally

i want to remember my body is a temple   floss my teeth

between you and me, i think of my teeth as representative of
my adolescence: my terrible effort toward perfection, my first
failure(s).

i do not dream of my husband. i dream of my past lovers &
sometimes their sisters. i dream of them in pajamas that don't fit.

i must be confused about my sexuality, these dreams of men
and women and their sisters. certainly i have enjoyed penetration
and the fat tongues of men. i think it is funny to say i am a gay
divorcee, although it still comes up in my dreams that i am
concerned about hell.

in the dream where i gave up women another man was my baby's
father and i instantly longed for all things lesbian, in particular
the gossip.

but back to my teeth. i had them straightened, for which i
gladly paid top dollar, and when finally i bit into an apple it was
as sexy as fingers.

maybe a little bit like eve's first bite. imagine her desire,
overwhelming enough to shun safety for information. a thin
line of juice trembling on her chin. lilith's little sister finally
coming into her own

(later when looking at photos of eve in her youth her loved
ones will flinch, shocked by the damage of such a short space in
time. how then she was as beautiful as a fashion model. eve
unrepentant as ever (the irony not lost on her) tells her
children, "hell's what you make of it.")

when i wanted to be older i wanted to be like that. like leanne
on the mechanical bull; serious, drunk, almost as good as
urban cowboy & not unaware of the consequences.

revisions on an utopian hope

Athena was born of her father's head
(let us be born of ourselves)

remember the time you dreamed
you were complete with your body
& flying
we are this much possibly

you live in the heart of my fingers as they sort through the day
my papers are the lemon of your neck
my computer smiles from the corners of your bluest eyes

when I think of being a good girl now
I think good
this is good

something dangerous has happened

the thing about this dream
is you chose to fly
despite all the watching
and you

rev. 1

another Holy Virgin

according to Greek tradition Athena was a thought in the back
of her dad's mind, occurring after he swallowed her mom,
Medusa, who was symbolized by the snake. tastes like chicken,
smells like fish. I mean to say that I've heard that snake tastes
like chicken. I saw it on television.

also according to Greek tradition chaste. smart but dry. like
 a drum which when exceedingly dry gives out a loud noise.
probably sarcastic and largely unadorned. obstinately abstinent.

so, to say that a daughter stems from the head of her father is not
to say anything new and marriage (medusa being our case in
point) has been for so many like Zeus' enormous stomach.
naturally, we should be at work on our own destiny, giving
birth, one might say, to ourselves.

to speak the obvious with such zeal is, at best, annoying.

rev. 2

what do dreams of flying portend?

well, in that moment you are not fragmented
not trapped in your brain
not trapped in the brain trapped in the stomach of your father
he who will abide no resistance until
the dream turns into a jet crashing before your eyes
burning on the edge of what looks like Victoria
and why are you dreaming of Victoria
what has Victoria to do with your life at all?

this is a dream of your fear of freedom

rev. 3

Live in the heart of my sorting fingers
Romance is the one who will not linger,
my papers are the lemon of your neck
If you knew this girl you'd know this is dreck.
It ain't love when it lasts a mere two weeks
We weren't suited she of whom I speak,
And so this sonnet is not writ for her
Nor is it my love which I must now cure;
Idealized lesbian love is a sham
No, I will not swallow it Sam-I-am.
Chicks are a pain in the ass, this I know
For my father told me so. *(hold for 3 beats)*

This isn't to say I don't love my wife
She's not the wife – I'm the wife – such is life.

rev. 4

there is danger
of violence, of rejection, of embarrassment
of complacency
a not happiness of disastrous proportions

we are recklessly close to burning
in an inferno of dullness

rev. 5

we are this much
possibly more or less
anything
is
despite you
and me

talk talk

sips her red wine from a plastic tumbler

she   it's pernicious
           fear
           and the politics of art
           where everyone is a cowboy
riding off into abstract sunsets

she pulls slowly on a cigarette tucks her might-have-been-just-
fucked hair behind her ear leans against the wood bench blows
smoke towards you like if you cough she would say oh sorry
and laugh about you later but not because she's cruel she just
forgot you didn't smoke

you   oh yeah

she   in my only black and white dream death was laughing at me
          he lit the orange blouse with a bic lighter
          don't ask me what that means

the gold tumbler clatters on the floor

you   well at least it's plastic

she   when's that fucking waiter gonna bring us another drink?

her lipstick has left its stain on a tooth

you lean across the table wipe it clean with your thumb
impossible to mollify she squints like she's bearing you a
grudge now you must act like nothing has happened her face
echoes itself

l'air du temps

I've been decorated [1]
in skirts and promises

I pull thin strips off
the shape of my heart
I am tired of speaking of everything
except what's important
I can remember sitting in the garden [2]
of my big sisters' arms

mother I am taking myself home
I am leaving behind your fear [3]
I pack only your courage
only your ability [4]
I am taking myself home
to juniper and mountains
woman and the everyday [5]

I am going to carry summer in my pocket
no turning back
I am more than an idea
I am thaw
I am lips thighs fingers
I am flesh
I am feast

---

[1] my dad signed up for ww2 at 17 because he was 6'3"   he learned to drink screech
& fall in the harbour   he wore a rosary the whole time   once in northern ireland
he and his buddy the mason started a brawl   he got a strip of medals

[2] we grew only potatoes   the concept of life with woman as garden can't
withstand the daily indignities of farts and 7 am alarm clocks

[3] i used to break apart her pills   lick the bitter coloured beads

[4] she said   when you lie down with pigs you become one

[5] made a really neat skirt tonight & did quite a good job on my diet
(diary: april 5/79)

I am taking myself [6]

on this sky I can walk
in amber shawls
in purples

beyond the reach of reason and coercion [7]

---

[6] blah blah blah

[7] not true

music appreciation

music (being an art form) has no hard & fast rules

quintessential
catholic girl
everything she's done is on t.v.

largo largo
adagio andante
presto con fouco

she ought to forget feeling
& not feeling forget thinking
(which inevitably brings her to the shrill end of the necessity of
fashion)
& not thinking recall the taste of corpulence
of salt & butter
of cellulite dimples

still up against the deeply rooted psychological feeling
what women do is not as cinematic as what men do
suited perhaps for the small screen
one that requires no interpretation

thirsty girl
seeks diabetic lover

if there be hope for a fat lass
it must lie in menopause & osteoporosis
catholic girl will finally breeze
perfect as a cover girl
already accustomed to oblivion
past the silver screen
into her golden age

she will shed starvation
adagio   andante

drink whole milk in her cafe au lait
drop her low impact aerobic class
croon to herself on the bus
shed her skin of fear
her tongue will sing her body
largo   largo

quickly and with fire
she will forget

why I hate bees

Francis almost died once. Patrick almost died once. I almost died twice and Maria Caputo almost took me with her a third time even though the water was only up to your boobs. Francis fell through the ice and lost his other sneaker for the rest of the year. He had to wear boots the whole time because we weren't supposed to go to the frog pond. Dad almost kicked his butt off.

Once I almost died because I went with Rolly on his son's motorcycle without a helmet. Rolly was plastered and we wiped out. I had a scab from my elbow to my wrist. No one got in shit that time because Rolly and Kay had invited us all to their cabin on the lake. We had a big horseshoe tournament. Mom and Kay had whiskey sours and after the fall I got all the cherries. Francis and Pat said it wasn't fair so Mom said, "Who said life is fair?"

The next time I almost died I got stung by a bee. I got hives everywhere and I'm pretty sure if I ever get stung again I'm dead. I don't know if it was a bee, a wasp, or a hornet that got me, so I don't believe in going barefoot. Not even to throw out the garbage. Anyway it's not hygienic.

Patrick fell off a ladder and knocked himself out cold. Maria loved Patrick and wanted to pick him some flowers. Flowers are a good place to get stung but Maria took my hand and kissed it please please please a thousand times to make me fall under her spell. The best flowers are by the creek where the retired Sisters live but Maria fell into the creek and she couldn't swim. She was screaming and swallowing water like she was in the middle of a lake so I jumped in to save her. She got boobs the year before and her T-shirt was stuck all around them.

But it was bad because she started pulling me under with the force of her panic. I remembered how Mom said people can drown even in water to their ankles. I was thinking I should leave her to die but I saw Patrick kiss her the day before so I put my hand in a fist (with my thumb on the outside like a boy the way Pat taught me) and I punched her in the face. That calmed her right down.

Then we took the flowers to Patrick who said "Thank you very much Maria." Like I was invisible.

peppermint

the colour
of your perfume is stronger
than your peppermint touch
your hands in my hair
falling into your breast kissing eyes

again she stands too close says i shouldn't buy crest
mda drips down our throats is stuck to our fingers we buy it
from that tired bleached out woman who is a friend of the fag
who lets us stay at his house   she says she is really into me but
she fucks him we hold hands on robson street & dance at the
dufferin she doesn't think i should shave my legs she doesn't
think I should go to work she says i should be here now at
night she and he say mmmm oh i pretend i'm asleep we get up
at eight and go out for breakfast on davie street at her place
we sleep in the alcove bodies held tight mda and skinny she
gives me mushrooms in chocolate she says she is so into me
reads from anais nin says i am a guilty catholic picks wild
raspberries says she is really into me

under the bellies of horses

besides guilt

besides guilt
another thing catholics do well Jim said is

       always now and at the hour of our
       we measure our lives by their little deaths

like when I first realized about time
I was at Dorothea Walker
then I was almost home walking my bike up Paret Road past
the cows where we took Matthew and he would yell cow! cow!
that time up the road from school was complete
earth had rolled slightly over & it would keep happening

how we lost & what was surrendered after fear
blew in our ears
fat tongue crammed in our mouths
shut us up

all sackcloth & ashes creeping
a chronicle of anticipation

it is of course consciousness that sets us apart

       we see it in a rainbow
       we see it in a star
       we see it in a sunset
       it is never very far

we smell the blood of the slaughterhouse
long before there are
plans to make a transition to the hereafter smooth

be prepared
do your duty
grin & bear it
good things come to those who wait
silence is golden

or how

he walked under the bellies of horses

he was cross eyed you know until they turned
his eyes but he never learned to
see   it's never me
                       because I pay attention
                       dick
                       jane
                       red
                       out
                       I know words before they are said
                       Good
                       Girl
                       something about pre-lingual learning
                       danger is lurking lurking
                       and space is what to fear

he's sleeping it off
stupid from too much or not enough
dumb enough to say it's me
                       when I am very good   VG
                       virgin   VG
                       honour roll   VG
                       daughter   VG

he is   unsatisfactory   X
something about pre-lingual learning
he missed
boundaries
the way he walks into my room thumbs my books reads the
paper Christina made me walks back pours out the tea and
says   don't you have honey?

cohesion
that's about keeping it together
I is We
We call us the two ones
everybody likes to tell that story

then he went to the hospital then he went home and told everyone else

as if I didn't know
like the night we were born dad was at the hockey game
they said right over the loudspeakers because it was Fort St.
John and   everyone knew each other   they said Marty
your wife just had twins   see him walking up the bleachers
spiked coffee in hand wearing his Fort St. John Flyers jacket
saying something like well I'll be damned or shit and 2 makes 4
everybody shaking his hand

before that I remember liking my blue skirt so much and Ingar
the psychic said we have been unhappy again like the night we
were born how I watched him how I hid behind all those
months how my mother cried not over me again for 30 years

I should say about myself that I pretended we weren't related
I should say about myself that I feel like an always wife and he
is the kind of dad we talk about in cars   I should say he is
looking for the back of his Father's hand and I am sick of husbands
I should say nothing
this is another forgetting

a good day

it was very sad the day we heard that dad would die but it was
also fun because all my friends came over and we went driving
in the blue toyota that kelly's sister terry drove
and i was the centre of attention
it was a day like a movie of the week

my dad is buried in kelowna with a great view of the golf
course especially chosen for him by the graveyard worker who
knew his voice from the radio

my brother has been running from my father to the Father for
almost half our lives   but i am on the honour roll and that's
a great relief once my dad cried and said he loved me
on a good day i believe that's true

the last time we got drunk together i was 17 and dad took me
to big white   i met this one legged vietnam vet there for
the slalom exhibition   we left about 1 am dad in his shit
kickers down the fresh snow incline and he wiped out so i
went behind to catch
all 205 lbs if he fell again and i wiped out taking him with me
he said i won't tell mom if you don't
the next day his bones sure hurt

we often laugh about that
like the time when he almost died in calgary instead of
kelowna
mj racing to the rockyview dad hanging out the window trying
to breathe
and liz in the back seat says   big poppa i had to go to
emergency when i got a pussy willow up my nose

my mother says

giving birth is pulling your top lip over the back of your head
she did it eight times
it's the kind of pain you forget

she says
which of you wouldn't be here now?

they planned only two
me the least of all
silent in the doctor's stethoscope
seven tunnelled minutes
after my collapsed lung brother
who's always fallen on the careless side of brave

so the doctor says
hang on dear you've got one more
my mother starts to cry
they have only
one high chair
one crib
one

this is not to say I wasn't loved

blue dodge Sunday

I made him promise not to tell but he did right after mass
he said from the back seat where they can't see our faces
we know there is no Santa
he said I told him and I did   I told him not to say

1. one day I will try to kill him

Now I am thinking of those athletes we watch during the
Olympics. The ones who sail across our television screens, legs
kicked apart leaping over hurdles. I did that once. Leapt over
toppled chairs. Flawless. Unencumbered by my weapon. A
knitting needle. No, a steak knife. Rage can provoke
perfection. Hatred, it seems, has its finer points.

2. after that dad will creak into death

Named Multiple Myeloma. In plain English, cancer of the
bone marrow. Painful, brittle and six years long.

3. mom & I will get our photos taken at Woolworth's dollar
booth

At the side of Bernard away from the lake. Where you can buy
cheap purses and scarves. Bonnie Belle roll-on lip gloss. Bubble
gum or strawberry flavour. Gone now, I suppose, to Walmart or
Zellers. I still dream I am shopping there. Sometimes with
Glenda.

he chases the burnt lip
life in a thin margin with
gaunt assistance of government & meds
the edge of his skin bumps into everything

I wish I could tell the future
then I would say to my brother
later when we play Sunday drive in the new front seat
that blue dodge lighter will burn your lip

our summer holiday at some pool when they called you fish

in the car
we said what is the opposite of up and mom said down
we said what is the opposite of boy and mom said girl
we said the opposite of me is you

when we play company
this is the way we laugh
        HaHaHa
        heads flung back
        teeth bared like the talking horse

when I play wife I play I am my mom
this is what I remember

        and because of how I cried everyone called me fish

this is what else:

you lay on the grass
watched the earth turn
feared distance
& the passage of time or perhaps
the construct of the passage of time

because either time rotates
(dad on his bed)
or it's a train
(mom & the living room t.v.)
whose doors open now   and now
it's beginning and it's never going to happen again
you becomes I

& my brain stops beating in my chest
I am a boy walking in the foothills
a boy walking in the foothills now
and now you would be a boy if I could make
illusory
memory

we're real because of this measurement of ink
and I becoming you cease to exist
like dad
who upon his death had clearly never been here at all
a figment of not imagination
although

I mean time is a cliche
and if I am a boy
I think I am not afraid
I am riding my bicycle quickly down a hill

and now I am in Calgary
in a tight red dress
walking downtown and it's hot and summer and
I'm a fearless boy racing a blue bike

I'm selling the *Albertan* in front of the Bay
extra extra
I'm on the scarsdale diet

if we are making a plan to leave perhaps
we are already gone

twelve & a half

we fall against the water   all in ears and over heads
port angeles   tacoma   olympia   spokane   lick chlorine
from our lips
hands pressed together for benediction
us red legs & belly

you say don't be afraid

because I want to dive

ordinary and small are we
except/and

nobody notices
you are so momentary

I clang through the surface pummelled and taut
one more discordant attempt

tired of so much noise you plunge
silent as peril the water collects

strange cities

facing west

everything in panorama

there are things that seem like silence; cars passing on an always somewhere highway, voices of boys calling out across the afternoon and Evelyn's chickadees chattering in the blue spruce. how terrifying, that blue spruce, when you imagine it crumpling – no, crashing – onto your roof. it would spell the end of you all, your grisly demise featured on the six o'clock news. families around their kitchen tables would click their tongues in horror. after that no one who'd ever loved you could sit under a blue spruce without feeling a pang. at your funeral all your ex-lovers would sit in a row. humbled by your sudden death. and a little bit destroyed. because there is was no one like you. they realize that now. and good, you think, they figured that out. except you won't be thinking. you won't be. you will be ashes for the compost heap. and that makes you not fearless, but dizzy. it makes you want to scream or puke or have intercourse. because of the force with which you can be pushed against a bed. because of friction.

this is a moment that can not be controlled

everything inside you is a weed

washed in the panic of nothingness you understand. not yourself, but what it is that takes strangers to public washrooms their hands stroking their genitals. not love, just that instant of being perfectly alive with no attachment to another. and no idea of the consequences of a blue spruce ringing with chickadees

strange cities

forget strange cities
the shape of your mother's sunglasses when she turned to look
the camping trip on the banks of the peace when you weren't yet
& your sisters in their thick cotton swimsuits

now it is Monday
pantyhose grip the corners of your thighs
cross & uncross the business of the day
what was it your father held in his hand in that photo
a fishing pole or a whiskey jack?

assets + liabilities = the net worth of a life

everything girl clatters past the corner of your eye
bangs the photocopier   fails to understand the delicate microchip
how it functions best when not subject to her violent insistence

tall as Jesus   flight of fancy
she is making the world safe for job costing
centering the universe to hover here under diesel
your father never held a bird in his hand

it's how the wage draws you in
each day you become more faxed jokes and girlie pictures
why don't women need watches?
less from where you were
that rocky beach on the banks of a river
the last place your mother camped
you are of this office
beiged and voiceless
except for the lilted good morning   good afternoon
you give good phone

on Mondays you reconcile payables
your sisters now a vague impression against the beach
you are must earn a living
this is where you live
now
you
must

forget the shape of your mother's sunglasses circa 1961

dearth

we are blind to the lotus of our mother's feet
become longing   become wishful

exacts of cost:
per cent of interest and lack thereof
investment divestment
binge & purge
when does selfishness become the saint

everything here is strange enough to be typical

magpie plunders crow
a sport utility scurries by
we expect too little   too few times
mutilate the flesh   in search of bones

a metaphor of loss or does it mean she's coming into money
this is the idle chatter of scavenger and corpse
become longing   become wishful

televisions are tuned to shows called hope and blue
such devotion flows eternal as plutonium

under sedation skin tolerates
enough to do a mother proud

in that space between fall and winter
that grey one of leafless and wind chill
skin waits   to be
                                 exhumed
                                 excused
                                 afflicted
                                 discovered
                                 chosen
                                 by:
                                      a)
                                      b)
                                      c) god

luna

February 5 1993 the moon was closer to earth than it will be
for another 10,000 years and I didn't even notice
I hate myself for missing things
February 5 1993 passed by
I couldn't say for certain what I was looking at
if it was the sky
February 5 1993 was 17 days before Uncle Gordon died
but I thought for sure he'd make it to summer
February 5 1993 my brother was likely dishing out some
bullshit line
maybe that's the day he was driving down a back alley & hit a
cyclist
February 5 1993 I started to believe he was born that way
that he was like my Uncle Gordon who couldn't relate to people
because my brother can't do anything right

I saw what happened and I felt the rest
it crept around the house
his sacrifice to a family's good name
but nobody says why
and I hate myself

I'd like to see the moon change that

x

generation exasperation exaggeration waiting waiting still
separating obligation expectation frustration education
cooking cleaning find a meaning
gender bender sex starvation weddings babies no yes maybe
race is running skin & history what comes next is a t.v. mystery
ranting raving & still you're craving coffee cancer smoke your
answer

popcorn toast & scrambled eggs thigh buster gets you better legs
$ninety nine ninety five is all you need to stay alive
heaven hell & jesus christ the religion of power isn't nice
thrill shopping power walking pistol packing dudes (ask them
what they mean when they use the word choose)
go straight to jail do not pass go do not look back or you'll
turn to stone

you're on your own you've got your health but what's a man if
he ain't got wealth? (if this screws you up cause you're a gyrl
joke's on you honey it's still a man's world)
what's her age she'll never tell oil of olay is her all weather shell

no fear my dear no fear no fear now is here stay cool stay clear
wagons ho! and all that shit move forward grrrl bit by bit
don't isolate   evaluate   initiate   elucidate
occasionally hesitate

fish bowl

a deer will kill your dog
if she can

what if you step out the door
and a deer is standing there
eating grass
looking at your dog

not bambi
it's the first thought that goes through your head

we're all a little bored and waiting
for tourists to spend their good money
we watch each other
t.v. and the weather

frightened by that which is missing
(dollars & sense)

winter still breathes down our necks
all wind and cloud coming up from montana
later this summer a bear cub will be caught in a village tree
surrounded by sidewalk and cameras

all the little sweetie pies will stand below her
waving to the folks back home

we're looking at some of the oldest exposed rock
undiminished by business and cliché
we watch each other
like each of us has something more real to lose

our dog barks at found bones left on the windowsill
they might be alive

new recreationist

Impossible to picture before the city moved in
9000 years ago
no polar fleece
too many trees most likely
nothing to do for fun
& nobody having gone to university.

Road development has brought us
some of thousands of others
to this to-do list of recreation
busy as a mall.

We are living in our
post-consumer recycled brain matter.   and
Today we are the discovery channel.   when
We are the new recreationists.   they
                                          were
In the 1950s a highway seemed   only
to make the world safer   half
daddies omnipotent   way
mommies delighted   up,
children obedient.   they
                                          were
In the 1990s a highway seemed   neither
to be a false gesture of connection;   up
unable to trust   nor
that navigating a vehicle   down
will turn us into neighbours
who borrow sugar.

archeological evidence suggests

We didn't lose our innocence
until the 1970s, right?
when a lot of us did drugs
& the energy crisis.

Now we do movies
& ride mountain bikes
in parks.

Getting back to nature as it were.

why maps don't

1. *

2. At the edge of the world a dog is herding rocks and
    everyone is laughing
3. Hunger is to blame
4. My body is a map dotted with ghost towns

5. Where should I have built the capital city
6. What should I have said
7. I'm not a cartographer!

8. Because of the force with which you can be pushed against
    a bed
9. Because of the first thought that goes through your head
10. Because of friction

11. I'm not even a gardener but apparently of garden variety
12. It's not about losing it's about defeat
13. What's the point of being a bush pilot if you're longing
    for respect

14. Mothers are trying to understand
15. Implicated by this turn of events
16. Somebody fucked up royally

17. Because of a spoon full of sugar
18. Because of what parents hope for
19. Because external & definite reality breeds

20. Contempt

---

* "We are through long familiarity, grounded in the assumption of an external,
objective, and definite reality, regardless of how much or how little we actually know
about it." David Lindley, *Where Does the Weirdness Go?*

life on earth as we know it

new as a christmas doll

in a prone position
place the infant against your chest
as if his weight can hold you in place
against the momentum
as if his racing heart
will lend language to this juncture

sleep
supercalifragilistic
monastic
retreat
apple
day
matisse
sinatra
power yoga
gray matter
hair
jesus
santa
expialidocious
latch
bath time
sleep
desire
snooze
christ
lady

each christmas you got a new doll
hair styled just like a lady's
sweet and plastic smelling

sign of the times

jesus in a baseball cap flips you a sign
hang loose
he might be walking to the park
sans disciples
incognito as it were

giddy with exaltation
the dog bounces
wet nose against the window
& the baby new as a christmas doll
full of rear-facing lonely
screams

toward jesus
with whom the dog could walk
on the water

jesus sports nikes
previously worn by a pronator
air salvation army
worn thin by so much of so little

he talks to himself
waves a hand in the air
stops to roll a cigarette

the driver behind you bruises his car's horn
words fly out his window
jesus   christ   lady

& you turn left
away from the man who your dog knows as jesus
lighting a cigarette in front of the big houses across from the park

after that she got fat

because we possess nothing &
she has less to say she begins

says:

chocolate is lettuce and she is a rabbit
knows she is a metaphor

she is a rabbit who taxis her bunnies to and fro
she is a nursery rhyme

chocolate is lettuce and she is rabbit
smaller in your hands than you would expect
even after you can roll her flesh between your palms
even after her body becomes a pungent curtain

she says to the baby "banana"
he replies "nanana"

she points out
he has six teeth

the better to eat you up with she whispers

better to eat you up

you should tell the baby
reality only becomes real when measured
thus, who holds the ruler is the equation

instead you tell him
what does the doggy say
woof woof woof

woof woof woof
the baby says
lips pursed into a kiss

he clicks his teeth
with the advent of language

woof woof woof
ma ma

sweet and plastic smelling

birds taunt one another
the rhythm of their jeers:
no rest for the wicked

you light another cigarette

the baby lurches toward the robins
aaaaah!   aaaaah!
he calls
the birds scatter
dubious of his gift for language

last night
blade sliced your arms
reminding you there is still a body
below the whirling mass of terrible energy
otherwise known as brain

the day is ringing in your ears
nasty

your skin
thin as paper

day ringing nasty

baby shatters your surface
a windshield clipped by a truck's rock

trrrru! he yells
growls his r's
that's right baby, you say
truck

you turn your arms with the steering wheel
& your flesh falls
so many pieces on the floor
strewn amongst cheerios

out flies your adolescence
snapping through the car
loud gum in your ear
its venom straightens your spine

the problem with cutting
is that which escapes
nattering
nattering

reminding you
how will you pull yourself together?

as always caught

probably not that smoking jesus

but 1 in 600 women
are fancy with scars
presumably

getting tired
of watching reasons
on Oprah

cut the skin
that sin
might be absolved

embody the confessional of life on earth as we know it

life on earth as we know it

in a prone position place the infant against your chest
as if his weight   his racing heart
can hold you in place against the momentum of time

the year you were born there was a record snowfall
travelers inched toward suppertime   your dad
wore a crew cut gray at the temples   slammed
the door too hard and the shoulder dissolved
dad & car tumbling through surprised space
earlier that year they woke your sister up to see
the dancing bear on ed sullivan
dad let her sip from his beer bottle & everyone laughed
that was the year your mother was going to learn how to drive
but after that she got fat & stopped wearing make up
once your sister told you your dad's breath was tar & nicotine
and not very nice

the baby is not enough to stop
your brain from splashing into the room
on the ceiling your brain look like a field of mice caught
in a record snowfall

remember to tell the baby not to talk to strangers

when we

think

inside a very (baby) blue shrine

those plastic xmas candles you put in a yard
real flame is a hazard

a mirror ball [1]

and the likeness of your chosen mother

she has a beatific stance

---

[1] like a diamond in the sky

entrance
antiphon

I had a little hen, the prettiest ever seen

surprising you say how alike the fantasies you & a lesbian have
& they do look similar still
you're looking for a wife or you've got one

not like your mom necessarily
more hip more dirty than her but finally
acquiescent

she washed up the dishes and kept the house clean

one thing about a lesbian
although not always clear to the common eye
she can be entirely different and exactly the same as you
lipstick and butch are not male & female
penetration is not necessarily hetero
and homo is not just sex

she baked me my bread
she brewed me my ale

she lives against the idea of being a girl

she sat by the fire and told a fine tale

catch?

penitential
rite

remember?
your mercy   your tenderness

because you sinned through your own fault
in your thoughts and in your words in what you did
and what you failed to do

when you were a girl

the BlessedMaryEverVirgin & all the angels and saints
would say:
stay out of the sun   put on your hat
your friend cuts her hair too short
why would anyone want to look like that

hey victoria 3 sheets to the wind & counting   *hear our prayer*
monica who can't recall the year she turned 12   *hear*
carol and marie discovering   *our prayer*

pour clean water on her
wash away her sins
prove her holiness
give her new spirit

I confess to you my brothers & sisters
I was looking for love in all the wrong places

novena

angels angels everywhere
and not a drop to drink

mother is angry
she sits at the kitchen table dipping her toast in syrup
another day when everything inside her is giving shit to life
listen jude
the whole company of heaven is coming to dinner
and she's taken a vow of silence
a valium and a little time away from it all
Our Lady of Macaroni & Cheese believes in miracles
if they don't happen at her house

she says it's better to be safe than sorry
as though the first precludes the second

each individual has an awesome responsibility for her
eternal destiny

in terms of the co-redemptive co-dependent infinite
   immaculate

and love means never having to say you're sorry [2]

hyperdulia

love is a mini splintered thing

another mom creamy as a statue of the holy one

blue eyebrows drawn on herself
a daughter who says you will go to hell
a son who is a spy, a puncher & a feeler down

one day she was drawing her face in the mirror and she
turned and said
(this is when you should describe the short hallway to
where she stood in front of the mirror, you with your bare
feet against the wood floor, chunks of whatever wasn't
vacuumed stuck to the hard edge of your heel. you have
never seen such boobs as hers, firm as lemons. her
daughter, too loud, is incapable of understanding)
get outside both of you. Now.

love means never having
a rose is a
skin in the tightness of all the wrong places

your mother says
don't let your tongue cut your throat

---

[2] she whipped them all soundly.

some advice

A little bit of information can be a terrible thing.
The rose is the flower of venus is the vulva and a marian
symbol of devotion. Preoccupation with a flowering rose
could lead to a rapid understanding the best person to do it
with is yourself. Do not think of this. It may not be a good
idea to make yourself happy on this earth. You won't know
until it's too late.

Think of nothing.
Try not to let eternity give you an anxiety attack. There are
things that are better left unsaid. Maybe the world really is
ending faster than you think & cars will be left driving
down Shaganappi Trail with no bodies because those drivers
knew better & they've gone to join Christ who you always
thought hung out with whores and tax collectors & was
killed by those self righteous

do unto others as you would have them do unto you
we beat the shit out of ourselves

(maybe you should get married)

liturgy of the word
first reading
a reading from a book of her mother's

First the Good Housekeeping one page story

how good it is to be a mother
and a wife

Then the Good Housekeeping novella

how good it is to be a girlfriend
then a wife

Redbook Ladies' Home Journal Family Circle
  Chatelaine Cosmo

Jeff[3], my husband, had to fly out of town for the week on
business. Madeline, an old friend from college, was coming to
visit me. It had been almost ten years since we'd last seen each
other. Madeline stepped off the plane as glamorous as ever.
Her shoulder length brown hair fell softly against her
shoulders. She was wearing a cream silk blouse and black wide
legged slacks. She strode confidently across the tarmac in a
pair of precariously high heeled shoes. Her long fingernails
were painted fire engine red to match her plump lips.

All this before lesbian chic and the popular return of the gay girl

Back at home I poured us each a glass of white wine and we
began the delightful work of catching up on each other's
lives. Much to my surprise Madeline informed me that she
had just ended a long affair with a woman, and this wasn't
her first affair with a woman. Madeline was a lesbian!

Hmmmm...

Naturally, at first I was a little shocked but then my curiosity
grew. What did she mean by lesbian? What was it like? Well,
as the evening wore on and we ate dinner and drank more
wine I found these questions burning on my tongue

buried embers may turn to flame.

and finally I asked her. What was it like to kiss a woman?

---

[3] The names have been changed to protect the identities of the people involved in
the events described in this article. S. Jones is a pseudonym for a New Mexico
based author.

Here let me show you

she said.

I don't remember the rest of the article. Except that for the remainder of the week while S. Jones' husband was away on business

the mice played

and nobody could tell by looking at them. When the week was over Madeline left and Jeff arrived. Madeline cured of her broken heart. S. Jones to continue her wifely life. The next day I told Anna and Vicky about the article, about women having sex together and they said

responsorial psalm

Euuuw!

grade seven

The year you were confirmed
The year I changed my name to Rose
The year I learned the tightness of my skin

A Christian practices the virtue of chastity by resisting lustful desires and temptations, rejecting masturbation and indecent entertainment of every kind.

Like none of us have heard that before
Sexual passion fuels the fires of hell

Most merciful Mother grant me purity of soul
Grant me straight teeth

At night I hold my hands tight between my knees
Waiting for a sign. A finger of truth
O beautiful most holy One, O perfect teeth and zitless face

Most merciful Mother grant me purity of soul
Grant me small thighs

My skin is a rash no one can see
I wish I had a date
Then I think of nothing and do it fast
I say better half a loaf than none at all

Most Merciful Mother grant me purity of soul
Grant my mom doesn't come home 'til late

My heart is in the right place

your fingers are in the wrong place

second reading
a reading from the book of Kinsey

Kinsey's Heterosexual – Homosexual Rating Scale

0	1	2	3	4	5	6

0 Exclusively heterosexual
1 Predominantly heterosexual; and only incidentally homosexual
2 Predominantly heterosexual; more than incidentally homosexual
3 Equally heterosexual and homosexual
4 Predominantly homosexual; more than incidentally heterosexual
5 Predominantly homosexual; and only incidentally heterosexual
6 Exclusively homosexual

Variables to Consider

1. Sexual attraction
2. Behaviour
3. Fantasies
4. Emotional preference
5. Social preference
6. Self-identification
7. Hetero / gay lifestyles

acclamation

O
Thank God

homily

At this point one should like to introduce the questions of
interpretation and choice. Is it necessary to enter into a
detailed description of self-gratification as experienced by
an adolescent woman or to simply allude to it? What is
accomplished by describing how you held a mirror to your

cunt, black hole, slippery, cave

Right. To discover the complex structure of damp folding
skin you've never really seen before. And how upon
reaching in there you encountered sensation. Now, having
just read that book about the 16 year old heroin addict who
masturbated with a pencil, you weren't exactly surprised to
feel something. You were actually quite determined.

slimy, stinky, fish hole

This determination reflected itself in a series of ways in your own sexual experimentation. For instance, you never had a visual image to go with your orgasm, I mean it wasn't as though you exactly saw rockets. It wasn't as though you lost control. It wasn't like Wicked Loving Lies when the heroine, I think her name was Marissa, is being raped by (probably) Dominic Challenger and even though she's resisting him she has this incredible orgasm against her will.

garage, box, scabbard, gash

You just made this contained space like the darkness behind your eyes and you whacked off. Secondly, you could do it in minutes – in less time than it takes to boil an egg. 3 minutes max. This proved to be a useful accomplishment in some later sexual encounters with men. Yeah yeah. Not all. So you could do it fast and you didn't really think you were doing it. But you did it a lot. The reason you didn't think you were doing it was because you didn't experience this spiral moving across your body. It was really a brain thing like a sneeze that just for one second let your brain stop thinking and feel. Just feel. And you could fall asleep immediately after. So it didn't matter if it was perfect. It was irresistible.

front bummy

And you were always in control. So the bed didn't squeak. So you'd hear someone come down the hall. So no sound came from your throat. So you could lie still the moment you heard a noise. And it was very vaginal. Not clitoral. You didn't realize about the clitoris for like, ten more years. But it's not a big turn on. It wouldn't be worth seeing. It was very business like. Hardly pleasure at all.

profession of faith

- I believe some things are meant to be. (That's not to be heard as an excuse for the systems of dominance that permeate the basic structure of our society)
- I believe you get more flies with sugar than you do with shit
- I believe in the luck of the Irish
- I believe there's a hair stuck between my teeth
- I believe woman-on-woman is far less objectionable than man-on-man
- I believe most guys see it as a turn on
- I believe it's true that lesbians were the hula hoops of the nineties

  If say, you're a lesbian

prayer of the faithful (why god made little girls)

God made the world with its towering trees
Majestic mountains and restless seas,
Then He paused and said, "It needs one more thing –
Someone to laugh and dance and sing
To walk in the woods and gather flowers.
To commune with nature in quiet hours,"
So God created little girls
With laughing eyes and bouncing curls,
With joyful hearts and feminine wiles,
And when he'd completed the task He'd begun
He was pleased and proud of the job He'd done,
For the world, when seen through a little girl's eyes
Greatly resembles paradise.

hubba hubba

prayer over the gifts

The first time I saw Purple again she was eating an apple
A symbol of the Goddess' sacred heart of immortality
Eve's fruit of knowledge and like the rose,
Represented by the number five, also a marian symbol
The first time I saw Purple again she was wearing a light
blue sun dress

And her hands reached out like this

I remembered her from high school
Finally there she was eating the core of her apple

hubba hubba

Not really
It was more the idea of sex rather than the act

In the end it was very catholic

But

reformation

The mother of pearl Virgin mom made in her ceramics
class started to talk

She'd been a femme bottom all right, the perfect wife, the
docile replacement anything to make you like her pushing
against the little thing that hangs down at the top of her
throat making her gag holding her head too tight. She
spewed forth family, Sears cards and a Hudson's Bay coat
found at a church bazaar. She was the child second bride.
Sure of herself and stupid. She believed he would love to
satisfy her.

a little bit of knowledge is a terrible thing

I'll tell you this much without her he surely would've lost
his kingdom
She kept the family together
When no one was around he called her the boss
She kept a lid on things
She kept a stash of tranquillizers and anti-depressants
For ever and ever amen.

until she kicked the junk

Then what a gossip she turned out to be
She was furious
Anger was an apple core caught in her throat
fat old and ugly
anger was a bitch

Bark Bark

the truth

None of it had really been to her taste
She said it wasn't the motion it was the meat and she was a
vegetarian

She said her milk of kindness was past its due date
And she said a number of things she simply should have
kept to herself

Anger when not expressed at the appropriate time, in an
appropriate manner,
can lend itself to a rather venomous display

& who needs to be reminded of the trouble with snakes?

image (problem)

Basically
it had become impossible for her to complete anything
stemming from a tremendous anxiety that it wouldn't be
good enough for her reputation
the high cost of adoration

Oh, and the fall from grace
Now that was an odyssey
though hardly of epic proportions
it was simply common and painful
verified by   teen suicide rates
                 assault & battery
                 excommunication
                 and unsolicited opinion

                         yes indeed, she wanted her cake and to eat it too

she wanted it to a fault
she wanted what she didn't even need
she wanted little things like shoes and a good haircut and
she wanted _____ (fill in blank)
she wanted love
not that sugar coated shit
she wanted sex and war and holidays
she wanted to make her mother happy
perhaps

                                                        wait!

dog
ma

she wanted to change the way she dressed
she wanted to stop feeling stressed

wrap it tight
to remain compressed
depressed
oppressed
& soon enough not impressed

she especially wanted good bone
tiring licking, humping, dripping &
she didn't think she should say that out loud
sex
she did not want the disapproval of mothers and others sex
but it was time to

don't wait

sexless
mum
she'd had it up to here

litany

or should I say
she had the patience of a mother
which is not to say much
necessarily

Mrs. of all

wars
children
mortgages
bay cards
untrained dogs
picket fences

spankings
broken arms
anger
punishment
failings
burnt toast
shitty pants
grudges

p(r)ay for us

heaven & hell
& suddenly

boredom

she needed to replace her furnace
repair her washer
get a new motor [4]

so, to speak

becomes unspeakable

all she said was (whew)
"I want to exist
by a definition I create"
& the rhetoric hit the proverbial fan

madonna medusa
tomato tomato

"I want to structure, pathologize, objectify, vilify"

---

[4] home again, home again, jiggety jig

"I want to create a pseudo future a post-post-feminist post
  nuclear post"

&

unsolicited opinion

- My sister has good taste in women, what does she
  taste like?
- I keep hoping you're going to meet a man you like
- I remember when gay used to mean happy
- I don't think it's right but I can't judge it
- Which one is the wife?

this is the shut up voice
don't rock the boat. you get more flies with sugar than you
do with shit. it pays to be nice. what would your mother
say. such a pretty girl too.

to hell in a handbasket

she walks out (finally)
her hands stuffed into her pockets
clad in blue jeans, head tilted to the ceiling
gasps & titters escape from the room
light flashes from the mirrors & the door
closes

everyone watches her leave
but no one pays attention

denouement

she's eating her cake

madonna-medusa's income has dropped
plummeted in fact

her kids choose careful allies

nothing has changed & nothing is as it was

she is   still breathing
           thinking about going back to school
           always on the rag
           & marginally employed

she was "born without a future" and now the future's here
she never imagined herself out
side of expectation [5]

---

[5] I would if I could if I couldn't how could I?

epilogue

I want to be loved by you alone & nobody else but you

don't let your tongue cut your throat
remember mercy

things that stick to the eye:
a tatooed neo-nazi marching across a television screen
two women holding hands on fourth street
a bumper sticker that reads: "Don't follow me I'm lost too."

resist information
notice the difference   don't

hey, it's a structural thing
(madonna medusa)

we are not permitted to be family, common law or otherwise
but the bogus bogus family is all we want to be

boo boop be doo

Nancy Jo Cullen is a poet and playwright living in Calgary. She was co-founder of the woman-centred theatre, Maenad Productions, which produced five of her scripts. Since that time she has owned and operated a café in Waterton National Park, had two children and completed *Science Fiction Saint*, her first poetry book.